ALLIGATOR PANTS

WALKING BEYOND MY FAITH

TANIA KUEHN

 FriesenPress

Suite 300 - 990 Fort St
Victoria, BC, V8V 3K2
Canada

www.friesenpress.com

ISBN
978-1-5255-4597-9 (Hardcover)
978-1-5255-4598-6 (Paperback)
978-1-5255-4599-3 (eBook)

1. RELIGION, AGNOSTICISM

Distributed to the trade by The Ingram Book Company

TABLE OF CONTENTS

DEAR PARENTS OF CHILDREN WHO HAVE LEFT THE CHURCH
(March 2016)

Dear Parents of Children Who Have Left the Church,

I want to begin by saying, "I get it." I understand that this has been a source of concern for you, and I know it has caused much sadness for your family. There have been arguments and awkward visits and sleepless nights. I'm sorry that this situation has resulted in fences that seem impossible to climb. I know it's difficult.

Dear Family and Friends, Pastor, and Congregation,

I'm not trying to convince you to be like me. I don't have it all figured out. I could be completely wrong.

It's been about five years since I began asking big questions about Christianity. It wasn't my plan to go down a path that eventually led away from the faith; rather, a few questions started to pester me, and I simply couldn't drop them. I won't get into the details right now, but I'll just say that they were questions about God's intervention in the lives of His children, about His goodness ... and, eventually, about His existence. It's been about four years since I started shifting away from many of my former beliefs and rituals, and a year and a half since I last attended a church service. From a distance, it might look like this has been easy for me. For the most part, I'm still going about my life as usual. I work full-time, go on trips with friends, post "normal" things on Facebook, and have good relationships with my family members and friends. There's been a lot going on inside, and that's the part you cannot see. You might think I didn't lose one night of sleep over this. You might think that the shift—from devout Christian to doubting believer to "on the fence" to where I am now—was pretty straightforward and that I went about it light-heartedly. It wasn't, and I didn't. I didn't make up my mind one day that I'd had enough with the Christian religion and was dropping it. There was a lot of back-and-forth, a lot of re-thinking, a lot of double-checking my sources and asking the same questions over and over.

Of course, it's not just about me and my story. Many of us have left the church and the faith we were taught since we were little. We watched it crumble, and we didn't—we *couldn't*—stop it from crumbling. We tried other churches—the megachurch on the highway, the church that a co-worker recommended, the tiny thirty-member church around the corner, the modern churches, the old-fashioned ones. We struggled with almost everything that touched on religion. Eventually, we stopped trying so hard to make it all work. Maybe you think we've become lazy, careless, carefree. Maybe you think we're "getting back" at you, the church, or God. I know this isn't the case for me or for many others. Early in my deconversion, an acquaintance reminded me that what I was going through wasn't so much a spiritual issue as it was an intellectual one. If it turned out that God exists and is good, He'd accept me, inquisitiveness and all.

I can almost hear you becoming upset. I don't like that this is how things are right now, either. I imagine you're wondering, *Just what, exactly, is she saying here?* I'm saying, "You have not heard the whole story—my whole story, the stories of other people who have transitioned out of religion—because too many assumptions are preventing you from hearing it." Perhaps you're assuming that my faith wasn't real in the first place, that I wasn't ever a "true Christian." Perhaps you're assuming that I'm looking for attention, or that I'm just bored and looking for a way out. Maybe you think my words will destroy your faith, so you want to keep a safe distance from me.

When a person we love, especially a close family member or friend, leaves the faith, it's an uncomfortable, confusing, scary thing. We want to run away from the discomfort and fear. We want to put our hands over our ears and shut out the disturbances. We want to go back to "how things were" (and to that I would slowly nod my head and say, "I know… I do, too"). It's scary to ask questions you never thought you'd ask, like "Is God even there?" or "How can someone leave a faith that they held so close for so long?" or "What does all of this mean for life here on Earth, and for eternity?" Oh yes, those are HUGE questions! Sometimes, though, some of us can no longer settle for the answers we used to have. And it can be a scary journey. I know.

I'm trying to make it easier for all of us. I want to talk about the status of religious faith in my life right now. I want to hear the questions you have for me. I want to build bridges, not be kept at a safe distance where you don't have to enter my world.

Dear People in My Christian Circle,

We've left because, yes, we gave in to the voices that told us that it's okay to read, to research, to ask questions, and to not leave those questions alone. We've learned that curiosity is a healthy thing, and that it's okay to think through things critically. For each of us who has left, it's been a journey. Most of us probably read a lot and talked a lot—we found any way we could to inject the topic of religion into the conversation. We studied a lot. Prayed a lot. Watched videos. We learned about history, science, psychology, philosophy.

We read about the origins of our own religion and also of other religions. We read about other religions and compared those to Christianity. The Gilgamesh flood myth and the Osiris myths made us perform mental gymnastics. We saw the differences and the similarities. We questioned which religion was "more correct," which made more sense, which seemed to resonate or not resonate with our innermost being. We wondered if they could all be right ... or if they could all be wrong.

Once our research began, we couldn't drop it. With a mixture of fear and confusion, exhilaration and enlightenment, we pressed on. What would we lose from all of this? What would we gain? Most certainly, the world as we knew it would be disrupted, but how much? Where would this lead? Would this change us, our attitudes, our words, our actions?

We examined our hearts. Were we expecting too much from God? Did we have desperate urges to do sinful things all the time? Were we just frustrated with life and everything in life, including God? But no, none of those things seemed to be the problem. We wanted to believe. But we couldn't.

So many times we stood up to sing worship songs along with the rest of the congregation, but the emptiness overwhelmed us, and the words just didn't seem to make sense anymore. We tried to fake it, but that felt worse. We tried to stand silently while the music filled the room, and we listened to the voices around us, so confident and lively, while the voices in our own heads whispered, 'I can't do this anymore; I can't do this anymore."

We read about psychology—why we do what we do, why we believe what we believe. We read the lists of cognitive biases and logical fallacies, and we discovered how we used those to defend our own beliefs, rationally or otherwise. Slowly—or for some people, maybe not so slowly—some aspects of our faith began to fall to pieces. We questioned why the church emphasized certain things, like all the rules around sex. We were confused when we tried to figure out things such as creation and the Trinity. The Old Testament made even less sense than it did before. We wondered about the writers of the books of the Bible. We wondered what really inspired it all. We wondered about the role of power and control within the church, both now and in the past.

We delved into history. We read about the gods of the hunter-gatherers. We read about the agricultural revolution and ancient civilizations.

We read about the Roman Empire and Constantine. We read about the dying-and-rising gods of the Middle East. Divisions in the church. Scientists, explorers, popes. We wondered what would have happened if European colonizers hadn't brought their religion over to America. Would we be Christians? Would it be bad if we weren't? We looked at maps and timelines. We tried to put the pieces of the jigsaw puzzle together. Things fit differently than expected.

And we continued to look "outside the box." Speaking of that box … we started to see that it isn't wrong to doubt, to research, to let go of certain beliefs. We began to see that it was okay—healthy, even—to put things under the magnifying glass, to not accept everything on faith. We felt liberated when we could reveal to a co-worker or a hair-dresser some aspect of Christianity that no longer made sense to us, and then hear them reply, "Oh, I know what you mean!"

Dear parents and church-goers and pastor and Facebook friends, I've heard the gossip. I've heard about your concern. I've heard that you're praying for me, yet you haven't asked me why I left. You tell me that I have to "work on my relationship with God," that I need to "forgive those who have done hurtful things," and that "no church is perfect," but it's not about that. That's not why I left. I left because there are too many beliefs and rituals that no longer resonate with me. Love still resonates with me. Grace and forgiveness and "living with purpose" still resonate with me. Church does not. Organized religion does not. All the things that church offered to me, I've been able to find in other places. I know … that's a very vague thing to say. If you're curious, ask me. Email me. Call me. Make an effort with me instead of just talking about me.

Dear Church People,

As the years go on and I continue to journey out of religion, I still miss it sometimes. I miss some of you guys. I see your pictures on Facebook, or something reminds me of that chapter of my life, and some days I want to go running back. For the most part, though, I'm happy with my life now.

But if you call and invite me for lunch or to your summer barbecue, I'll probably take you up on that offer!

Take good care.

Tania K.

WORLDS APART

(November 2014)

A few weeks ago, I attended a Sunday morning service at my "home" church for the first time in a long time. I've now made the decision that I won't be going again for at least one year. Maybe in a year or so I'll be ready to try again, but for now, I can't do this anymore. I can't.

I went to the service with an open mind. Maybe this time I'd be okay. Maybe I wouldn't get frustrated, or disheartened, or baffled. Maybe I'd be able to pick out all the good parts of the service and ignore the rest.

I didn't intend to open the hymnal, read the title of the first hymn that we were about to sing, and slam it shut ... but that's what I did. In my head I was screaming for the hundredth time, *I don't agree! I can't sing this! This is NOT me anymore!* My family was sitting beside me. They sang, and the other people sang. I just bit my lip to keep from screaming or crying or both and tried to distract my mind with other things.

We stood for prayer because that's what we ... they ... do. They pray for those in the church, in the city, across the world. I stood, closed my eyes, bowed my head, and would rather have been out there—visiting someone in a nursing home, giving money to a homeless person who might not even really be homeless, reading *Psychology Today* magazine, or going for a long walk to clear my head.

And the pastor ... he preached. I don't remember much of what he preached. I just remember that at one point he made a comment about "the unbelievers," "the atheists." As though we chose this. As though we're selfish, unkind, lazy. As though this is an easy journey.

I tried to pay attention. I tried to follow along. I tried to give the benefit of the doubt. Did I just misinterpret his words? Was I being too sensitive? Was I over-thinking the words of the hymn? Were the prayers, perhaps, actually sincere? Maybe some people think that it's just as good as doing something.

And then we got up, sang another hymn, made small talk, and left the building.

After visiting with my family for a while, I drove home. I listened to the radio and reflected on the day. I opened the car window because it just got so warm. I couldn't focus, and I couldn't drive. I pulled over on the side of the highway, my throat sore from screaming, "I can't do this anymore! I absolutely cannot do this anymore."

Worlds apart—that's what was running through my head as they all sang and prayed and listened. Worlds apart.

The hymnal … the songs about God our Father, about our need to be rescued from our sinful nature, about how lost we all are just for being human …

The prayers … this attempt to care but to stay detached, to speak to God but not to physically reach out to His children, to leave things alone after "Amen" is spoken …

The sermon …

Worlds apart.

The words of condescension from a pastor who probably has no idea what it means to shed one's faith. Who probably has no idea how confusing and scary it is to lose that part of our identity. Who probably has no idea that sometimes it's no problem to sing along with verse one, but when it comes to verse two, three, or four, we're just shaking our heads at the absurdity of it all. Who probably has no idea how bizarre it is to realize one day that it's so much easier for us to relate to Sam Harris than to Billy Graham.

Worlds apart.

I cannot imagine saying goodbye to this church forever. It's been part of my life since I was a kid. For the last couple of years, I've had mixed emotions about it. I like the people, and I like certain parts of the service, yet it isn't me anymore. It hasn't been me for a long time. It's been three years since the start of my deconversion, and I now consider myself agnostic/leaning-towards-atheist. I still attend church with my family on some weekends; they know about my "struggles" and "doubts," but it's not something we talk about in much detail. I think I'm finally done trying to make others feel at ease by knowing that I'm at least still attending services.

I think also of the countless times I've sat there - baffled, empty, angered - thinking, *I can't do this anymore.* Weddings, funerals … that's it. Maybe in one year I'll give it another chance, but for now, I'm leaving that door closed.

I'll get in my car, and I'll drive out to the countryside. I'll find peace and comfort in the long stretches of road in front of me—in nature, in silence. I'll go for a walk on a cold night in the middle of winter and see snow falling around me and a full moon high above, and I'll be amazed by the beauty of it all. I'll go to work and my co-worker will tell a joke that has me doubled over, and I'll know that life is good. And maybe I'll have a really bad day next week, but a friend will email or call or hug me tightly. It might not be God or the church people or an unexplainable miracle, but for now, it'll be enough.

CONSIDERING THE DEPARTURE
(March 2017)

My job as a housekeeper at the hospital offers some insights into facts of life that are, for many people, unfamiliar and uncomfortable. After years of working in hospitals and nursing homes, most of it isn't a big deal for me anymore—these places of aging and sickness and healing, the hospital gowns and the bedpans, the bells and alarms that ring all day.

When working in a hospital or a nursing home, the thought of death isn't as distant as it is in other workplaces. In the unit I work in, death isn't as common as it is in other units. After surgery, most people are ready for discharge within two or three days. But every once in a while, that's not the case.

A few mornings ago, I was cleaning a patient's room, and her husband told me that death was imminent. He said that it might be in a few hours, or maybe a day or two. About two hours later, the patient passed away. Her husband told me the news, and I offered my condolences. I wasn't working nearby when the porters came to transfer the woman's body to the morgue, but I've seen it in the hallways a few times—the "blue stretcher." I cleaned the room afterwards, just like I've cleaned other rooms in which people spent their last moments. It's always a different sort of feeling when you know that this was it—the place where someone said their last words, breathed their last breaths, and closed their eyes for the last time.

Death is a huge topic. It can be awkward, scary, weird, a relief, beautiful, bittersweet. Being so close to it—seeing the butterfly sign on the door of a patient's room, talking to someone who has just lost a loved one, seeing the empty spaces afterwards—still makes me catch my breath sometimes.

For as long as I can remember, the topic of death was commonplace. I can't remember when I first learned about it ... probably from my parents or Sunday school. I'm sure there were some colouring sheets or a felt board that showed me what heaven and hell looked like. In heaven there were puffy clouds, bright lights, good little boys and girls, and Jesus. Hell was home to heat and fire and the devil, who looked like the Green Giant on a can of peas.

Those of us who grew up in the church are familiar with altar calls—the pastor's invitation to come to the front of the sanctuary and commit (or re-commit) one's life to God. I remember many pastors saying things like, "If you're uncertain about your salvation, please come forward to pray with someone here at the altar. If you're uncertain about where you're headed after you die, please come to the front. Are you sure you're going to heaven? What if you were to step out of this church tonight and get into a car accident and die? Please make sure you're on the right path. We're here to help you." Even as a teenager and in my early twenties, I never felt an urgent need to go forward to "be saved" from eternal damnation. Sometimes I'd whisper a heartfelt prayer to Jesus to make sure He and I were on good terms, and most of the time, we were. When we weren't, I'd pray extra hard and read extra chapters in the Bible until things were okay in my mind.

I really learned about dying and death between the ages of twenty-two and twenty-seven, when I volunteered with Shuswap Hospice Society in Salmon Arm, where I lived for a big part of my life. Here I was exposed to other views of death and the afterlife, not just the Christian view. It was valuable to learn about others' journeys, regardless of their religious faith. I learned about the experience of dying—what it looks like, how it varies from person to person, what people need, what's important in the days and hours leading up to death. I learned much about dying, death, and grief from the training sessions, the monthly volunteer meetings, the conferences, the program co-ordinator, and the hours of bedside vigil. I also learned to live life fully, here and now.

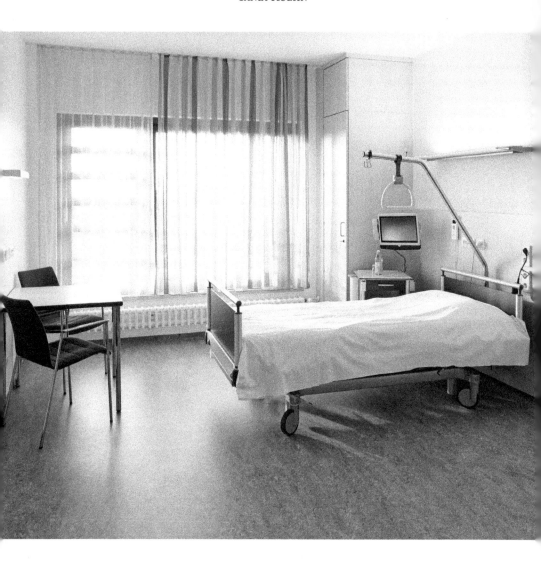

A few years ago, in 2012, I took a leave of absence from my job to take a funeral service program and work in a funeral home. The ten months I worked at a funeral home in Penticton were eye-opening and thought-provoking. It was interesting to see "what happens next." I'd sat at the bedsides of many hospice clients, but I didn't know what actually happened after they passed away. At my job at the funeral home, I'd ride along in the Town & Country van with my mentor or another staff member, and we'd transfer the bodies of the deceased from the place of death or a morgue to the funeral home. Occasionally I did transfers on my own, at all hours of the day and night. I worked with my mentor in the prep room, helping with washing, embalming, dressing, and casketing. The crematorium operator showed me the workings of the retort and the processing machine. I learned the paperwork end of things—vital statistics forms, obituaries, service folders, and so on. I sat in on arrangement interviews with my mentor and the families who needed funeral services. I didn't keep track of how many funerals or Celebration of Life services I attended during my time there, but probably twenty or thirty. I performed various tasks: seating people in the church or the community hall, helping the funeral directors wheel the casket to the front of the church, helping set up the lowering device at the cemetery, driving the hearse (just once or twice), filling in for a pallbearer, waiting at the gravesite after the guests walked away and before the cemetery staff came over to finish the task of burying the deceased. (I can go on and on once I start talking about my funeral home experience, so I'll save that for another time! I will recommend a few books, though.*)

In the last six years, since about age twenty-six, my transition away from Christianity and towards a non-religious/humanist worldview has brought about more changes in how I view death, life, the after-life, and all those "kind of a big deal" subjects. I've noticed that some people assume that I don't think about such things—as though leaving my religious faith has somehow made me shallow, unaware of things like my "salvation," or resigned to death as simply a cold, harsh reality. I would say this about my shift away from a religious belief system: I have just as many questions now—maybe even more—but I'm okay with that. I'm okay with saying, "I don't know what happens after we die." I care about how I live in this moment, this day, this lifetime. I'd rather put more effort into living my life as well as I can, here and now, than being overly worried or excited about an afterlife. There are enough things in my life right now that keep me challenged and working to improve some aspect of myself, or that keep my mind occupied in some other way. I don't have to dwell too far in the future.

For me, the subject of death often brings about feelings of curiosity, peace, stillness, relief that it's the end of the craziness we often have to put up with in this world. Of course, sometimes the thought of *others* dying terrifies me. When I think of losing any of the special people in my life, I wonder how much I'll cry, if I'll ever make it through Kubler-Ross's five stages of grief, and how I'll eventually pick up the pieces of my shattered world and carry on. I feel okay about the thought of my own death, but I hope it doesn't happen for a long time—I've got stuff to do here!

Sorting out all our feelings around death is a lifelong journey. We won't know how we'll handle someone else's death or our own death until we're actually there. Worrying about it or over-thinking it won't help. For now? Go out and live life!

*Three books from which I've learned a lot are *Smoke Gets in Your Eyes* by Caitlin Doughty, *Curtains* by Tom Jokinen, and *The Undertaking* by Thomas Lynch. I also really like Caitlin Doughty's YouTube channel, "Ask A Mortician." It's a bit kooky, but also funny and down-to-earth. This girl's passion about her job is obvious. I also like the children's book *Lifetimes* by Bryan Mellonie and Robert Ingpen. Some other helpful books related to dying, death, and grief are *I Wasn't Ready to Say Goodbye* by Brook Noel and Pamela Blair, and *Final Gifts* by Maggie Callanan.

BABY JESUS SEASON

(December 2015)

Baby Jesus Season will be here soon. In a few weeks, people will head out to Christmas church services, concerts, plays, potlucks, perhaps even a carolling session—all of which will be focussed on the birth of the Saviour of the world, the Messiah, the King of kings, the Lord of lords.

When I was a believer, I was all in. I was serious about it. Involved. Passionate. Even though the Christmas season has never been my favourite time of year, I still enjoyed participating in many of the Baby Jesus* festivities. Even now as I wear the "agnostic-leaning-towards-atheist" label, I look back on that chapter of my life and think about the good times.

I definitely loved the Christmas potlucks—the combination of home-cooked food, tons of people, decorations, and singing along with the old piano in the church basement. How could that not be a fun time? The carolling—a dozen or so of us youth packing into a few cars and driving to houses and nursing homes, singing a cappella and spreading holiday cheer to others. There were the endless Nativity displays at churches. And the concerts—not just one per season, but maybe two or three! Why not? The birth of our Saviour was kind of a big deal.

There were also quieter moments. One Christmas, a year or two before Christianity began slipping out of my grasp, a small church in my hometown needed a piano player for their service. I could play well enough to accompany the congregation as they sang "Angels from the Realms of Glory" and "Silent Night." Several times before the service, I picked up the church key from the janitor's house and went to the church to practise on the piano there. I loved the church music.

And then … and then … it all began slipping away. That hurt a lot. It seemed that the world was so dark and empty. What seemed so real and wonderful just … changed. My worldview crumbled, and I wasn't quite sure how to go about re-building. I couldn't pray anymore; my connection with God no longer felt strong, and it often seemed as though there was no connection at all. I couldn't sing the songs anymore. People's conversations about God seemed so foreign, because their God was so different from the one who was being revealed to me. I tried for a long time to keep it up, to keep trying, to give Christianity yet another chance, but still, it slipped away.

Some days, I feel like I could hold onto the sadness forever. I think that's understandable—after all, it's no small thing to lose one's religious faith. But then I'm reminded in a hundred ways how important it is to let go of what no longer works. Release. Move forward. Release some more. Ease up on the ruminating. There's no time limit for grief, but there comes a point when a person has to loosen their grip on the past, the sadness, the anger, especially when that grip no longer does anyone any good.

I'm slowly realizing that I've become occupied with other things. I can often remain emotionally distant from all these things that used to mean so much to me. Sometimes it takes a very conscious effort to occupy myself with other thoughts, and at other times it's just natural to move forward.

*Shortly after the start of my deconversion, I was chatting with my hairdresser. I knew from my previous appointments with him that he sang in a choir, so I asked him if the choir was performing a Christmas concert. He chuckled and remarked, "Oh! Baby Jesus Season! Yes, that's coming up, isn't it?" I still smile when I think of our chats as he cut and coloured my hair.

IF I WERE TO TELL YOU

(July 2016)

If I were to tell you that I no longer call myself a Christian, I hope that you'd pause for a minute. I hope that for a minute you'd suspend words and emotions and just … pause.

If I were to tell you that I no longer understand why such emphasis is placed on certain teachings in the Bible, I hope you'd know that I'm not talking about things like love, kindness, forgiveness, and all those good things. I'm talking about things like virgin births, resurrections from the dead, and other supposed miracles. I no longer think we must hold onto those teachings in order to be good human beings.

I might then tell you that it's been a year and half since I attended a Sunday morning service at the church where I grew up. That I'd decided on that day that I would take a break from church for at least a year, because it seemed too drastic to say I'd never go again. I'd tell you that it's been an interesting break. I've missed it like crazy; I've felt liberated; I've felt waves of anger and confusion; and I've smiled about the good ol' days. For many months after my decision to take a break, I'd drive past other churches and their full parking lots, and I'd get a lump in my throat, simultaneously wishing I could just go back to how things were yet knowing that the church experience no longer resonates with me. I'd tell you that I try to keep doors open and I try not to burn bridges, but also that I've learned that sometimes we need to let go.

If I were to tell you that I hadn't taken part in communion for years (even when I still semi-regularly attended church services), maybe you'd ask me why I chose not to take part. I'd tell you that when I read through the lists of "What Christians Believe," I couldn't honestly say, in my innermost being, that I held many of those things to be true. It no longer made sense to me to spend so much time and energy trying to figure it all out, to explain it to myself and to others. The Trinity, the creation story in the book of Genesis, the Easter story, Pontius Pilate, Virgin Mary … I just wasn't *there* anymore.

If I were to tell you that I hardly ever play worship songs on my piano, or that I can't muster up a prayer anymore, please know that there were innumerable times, especially early in my departure from religion, that this broke my heart. My special connection to God seemed so shaky when once it was so steadfast, so constant. It was no easy thing to feel it all slipping away from me; as time went on, I knew it wasn't "just a phase." The emptiness was overwhelming when I realized that my world was changing so much.

If I were to tell you about the long conversations I had with my co-worker Carl in the early days of my departure, you'd know the relief I felt knowing that I wasn't alone, that I wasn't crazy, that I wasn't the only one who had questions. Those talks rescued me in so many ways.

If I were to tell you that one of my closest friends is an atheist, it means that I've met a friendly, caring, interesting person who, as it turns out, hasn't believed in God for the majority of her adult life. If you were to ask what we talk about, I'd tell you that we talk about life and death, our hopes, our fears, our families, what we struggle with, and how we work through our struggles. I'd tell you that we talk about our pasts, our presents, our futures. The same kinds of things I'd talk about with family and friends within the Christian circle.

***

If your co-worker told you that she never prays, I hope you wouldn't criticize her. I hope you'd be curious and ask what she does instead. I wonder if you'd ask how she incorporates A.C.T.S. (Adoration, Confession, Thanksgiving, Supplication) into her life. I think you might be surprised at how she does these things, and I think that could lead to an interesting conversation between the two of you.

If your non-religious cousin were to tell you that he no longer gives 10 per cent to the church, I hope you could see the ways in which he contributes money, time, and effort to other organizations and projects. I hope you could see that he's trying his best … and that may or may not look like what a religious person does.

If you found out that your new neighbour is an atheist, I hope you'd remember what the Merriam-Webster and Oxford dictionaries say. I hope you'd see that immoral, lazy, unthinking, uncaring, and sinful are not synonyms for atheist, and that the definition of atheism is "lack of a belief in the existence of a God or gods." I hope you see that's all it is.

If you or I were to find out that someone doesn't believe what we believe, I hope that we'd just … pause for a minute.

WHITE SANDALS

(April 2012)

Sometimes well-meaning people teach us things that aren't true … things that, when scrutinized, don't stand the test of time. Stories that turn out to be untrue. Rules that can, in fact, be broken, without resulting in a catastrophe for all parties involved. Suggestions for "a better life" that often don't lead to a better life. I'm reminded of the *white sandals* incident.

Three years ago, my family attended a wedding. The ceremony took place outdoors, in a park. It was a hot day in mid-July. The bride was beautiful, the groom was handsome, and love was in the air. After the ceremony, there was a two- or three-hour break until the reception, so I offered to take my sister to the beach. My sister has some cognitive disabilities, and she functions at an age three level, even though she's just a year younger than me. We drove the short distance to the beach. I was wearing a black and pink dress and strappy black sandals with heels. I realized she was wearing white sandals. I didn't want her to get the sandals dirty in the sand, so I told her to take them off. I might have even offered to carry them.

We walked past people who were sun-tanning, playing volleyball, and swimming. A man lying on a towel stopped me and asked if it was too hot for my sister to be walking in the sand. I didn't know. She hadn't said a thing. I forget sometimes that she'll go along with almost anything anyone tells her. She's just like that. I don't go to beaches that often, so it didn't occur to me that the sand might be scorching. I thought I was doing a good thing, as I didn't want my sister to get her sandals dirty. I didn't think for a second that her feet might be hurting.

That's how I now see many of the things I was taught over the years by pastors, teachers, leaders, parents, and friends. They had good intentions. We grow up with certain ideas and we don't really question them. We get set in our ways, and we're surrounded by people with similar ideas. After a while, we don't even realize what we're doing or why. Then we pass someone who asks whether we think the sand is too hot to be walking on.

Having our faith questioned, doubted, scrutinized, and shattered is definitely not so easy to "fix" as slipping on those sandals and continuing a stroll on the beach. The thought-processing, the re-prioritizing, the sleepless nights, the searching, and the lack of answers … none of it is easy. But here we go. Maybe one sandal is on already.

RE-VISITING THE CHURCH:
THE DAY BEFORE
(April 2017)

In about twenty-four hours, I'll set foot in the church I took a break from over two years ago. I'm going for a special wedding anniversary that will be acknowledged during the service with the presentation of a plaque to the celebrating couple. I'm filled with mixed emotions: curiosity, worry, detachment, indifference. The last time I attended the church, I told myself that I wouldn't go back for a while, except maybe for weddings and funerals. I think this occasion counts as something similar to a wedding, so I'll go.

On that last visit, in November of 2014, I'd been transitioning away from Christianity for over three years. During those years, I'd sometimes go to church on Sundays and then to Skeptics in the Pub on Mondays. I spent a lot of time in an online support group for deconverting Christians, but I'd still listen to worship music quite often. I tried other churches from time to time, making sure I'd covered all bases, yet deep inside I knew it wasn't a matter of finding the "right" church. I knew that my reasons for leaving had more to do with the religion in general and less with a specific place of worship.

On that Sunday morning, I'd given this church a chance (see "Worlds Apart"). I didn't sing along with the hymns, because I didn't agree with many of the words. I stood for prayer and listened to the choir and the sermon. That day the pastor talked about "Those people who don't believe anymore … who have hardened their hearts towards God … those who are agnostics and atheists." I tried to let it slide. I tried to remind myself that the pastor didn't know what he was talking about, that he wasn't informed, that he was closed-minded or self-righteous. I tried to listen to the rest of the sermon, but I was distracted and upset. The people sitting around me seemed unbothered. I felt so alone in the middle of all those "good believers." Even though I wasn't pretending to be in agreement with the service—I was just attending with the rest of my family, like a "good" daughter or sister would—I kind of felt like a hypocrite.

That evening driving home, I reflected on the church service. I knew my screaming and crying wasn't healthy, and I knew enough by then to realize that *I wasn't the problem.* It wasn't my shortcoming, my sin, my lack of faith or patience, or whatever. It seemed too drastic to say I'd never go back, but I'd promised myself to take a break from this church for one year.

A lot happened during that one-year break. I became more involved with the humanist organization, Centre for Inquiry (CFI). I went for many long walks in unfamiliar parts of the city. I made a couple of new friends. I wrote about my struggles with Christianity. I had a Sunday morning off work in the spring of 2015, so I went to a church service at one of the mega-churches in Kelowna. I ended up walking out halfway through. I went out for coffee, read a few chapters of a book, and went for a drive up to Big White. It was a lovely day. I continued with my singing lessons, which were a good challenge and kept my mind occupied. I met a wonderful man who helped me to become a bit more hopeful and calm and silly. I learned to let go a bit.

The end of the one-year break came and went, and I decided to extend it. By this time, I even felt ready to help other people who were struggling with the role of Christianity (or another religion) in their lives, so I took some training to become a volunteer with the Recovering from Religion hotline. I didn't finish the training, but I learned a lot through the website and the volunteer manual. In June of 2016, two other women from CFI and I started the Leaving Religion/Living without Religion peer support group here in Kelowna. We meet once a month to share our struggles with religion and help each other through those struggles. The aim of the group isn't to deconvert anyone, but to arrive at a place where we're healthy, happy, and purposeful in our journey, no matter what belief system we choose to follow.

And now I sit here and think about tomorrow, when I'll visit my home church after more than two years. I think about other things in life that I've moved on from: an old boyfriend or two, a university program, a friendship that fell apart painfully but necessarily, an obsession with my weight. I think, *Maybe I needed those things in my life at the time, but I'm done with them now.* I've seen other people and places. I've listened to other voices. I've cried enough, and I can look at those things now and see the bigger picture around them … and realize it's time to let go.

I think about that girl who sat next to her family in church over two years ago, feeling alone, confused, bombarded with all these things that no longer made sense. And I think of this year, this month, this day, and how I'm no longer *that girl*. I think I'll wear dangly earrings tomorrow and keep my hair down instead of pinning it up like I did for most of my church life. I'll listen to what's going on during the service, but I won't give it too much significance unless it makes sense to me. I think of how I'll have lunch with my family afterwards, and then eventually head back home. This time, maybe … probably … it'll just be a pleasant drive home.

RE-VISITING THE CHURCH:
A FEW WEEKS LATER
(May 2017)

On the first Sunday of April, I went to my "home" church for the first time in over two years (see "Re-visiting the Church: The Day Before"). I wanted to be there with my family for a special wedding anniversary that was being celebrated that month.

Going to a special event such as this isn't usually a big deal. I've been to a dozen weddings and countless funerals, bridal and baby showers, and baptismal services. I've been to hundreds of church services at many different churches. This time, however, was different. Over the course of the last six years, my transition away from Christianity has also included a big step away from the church where I grew up.

I felt a bit awkward on that Sunday morning but also comforted knowing that I'd be surrounded by my immediate family and some members of my extended family. (Although my immediate family does not always "get" my deconversion, they do love and support me and are trying to understand my situation.) As planned, I wore fancy earrings and kept my hair down, which is something I never used to do. I also safety-pinned the V-neck of my shirt, because it was just a tad too low, according to my "good Christian girl" background.

I entered the building and was immediately greeted with the expected, "Tania! Haven't seen you in a long time!" "How ARE you?" "Good to see you." It was nice to see some of the people again and not feel like a stranger, but it also felt superficial. A million things have happened since I last went inside the church over two years ago, and my "place" there is so different now than it used to be.

I stuck to the "socially acceptable" thing to do in situations like this—I smiled and kept my answers brief: "Oh, I'm doing all right … yes, still living in Kelowna … finally have a weekend off … crazy how time flies, isn't it?" It wasn't exactly the time or the place to launch into a big spiel about the challenges of leaving church, or about cognitive biases and logical fallacies, or the place of Christianity in the Roman Empire. Or how the whole thing no longer makes sense to me.

As we walked into the sanctuary, a few people played worship music at the front. As I sat down in my "usual" pew and took in the surroundings, my thoughts floated, interestingly, to the kitchen table of a good friend of mine. I choked up a bit as I recalled the hours and hours we spent there wondering, confessing, crying, and laughing about our similar experiences of leaving behind our religious faith. We'd talk about the challenges, the new insights, the bizarre things we no longer believe or emphasize so strongly. Sitting in the pew that morning, I thought about the many times, especially at the beginning of my deconversion, when I could open up to that friend or other acquaintances or co-workers and say, "Oh wow, you think that way too?" I could share with them that I no longer felt like God was real to me, and that my relationship with Him had seemed too one-sided for too long. I could admit that I was exhausted when my prayers seemed to go nowhere. I never really worried too much that I was headed to hell because of my crumbling faith or anything that I did or didn't do in my life, but every once in a while some of that preaching of guilt and fear did seep in. I thought about those conversations, however brief they were, that helped me navigate the world as my Christian faith slipped away. They helped me realize that I was not alone or completely crazy, and that I might eventually be okay.

After the introductory music, we listened to the announcements and sang some hymns. (I held my hymnal open to the appropriate page, but did not sing along.) The choir sang beautifully, as usual, and then the wedding anniversary was acknowledged with a plaque and a special song by the choir.

The sermon was based on John 9, about a blind man who was healed by Jesus. The pastor talked about people being blind and, more specifically, "spiritually blind." He talked about being receptive to the light that comes from God and the importance of abandoning the darkness that comes from all those worldly things out there. It was interesting to observe my own reaction to the sermon and to compare it to the way in which the pre-deconversion Tania would have reacted. I've learned to take things (such as this sermon) more lightly and to question authority figures, such as pastors. I see now that they're regular human beings, and what they and other people think about my life doesn't really matter. I'm beginning to understand that no one knows how best to handle every situation in life. Just because a person has a high position or a lot of education doesn't necessarily mean they have life more "figured out" than anyone else. I'm beginning to see the bigger picture, to decide for myself how much weight to give to others' opinions, and, ultimately, how to live my own life.

We had lunch in the church basement after the service. I mostly talked with my family, although I did chat with others here and there. My parents drove me back to Kelowna after the service and, relieved and content, I carried on with the day.

Even though I most likely won't go back to that faith, I'm grateful for the many ways it permeated my life. The church community was a comfortable "home," and I'm grateful for many of the wonderful people I met there. In the church, there's a sense that everyone has these big things in common—beliefs about God, Jesus, salvation, and the afterlife—and people seem connected immediately because of that. Even though I belong to a few other organizations now, I still miss the deep connection, however misinterpreted, that I felt with the church people. The holiday celebrations were a bit more special when there was that sacred feeling, that feeling of the supernatural, the rich history, and the beautiful music. I'd love to go back to whole-heartedly singing worship songs or feeling the power of prayer, but armed with all the information I have now, I don't think that will ever happen. I'd love to believe in the heaven I used to believe in—such a comforting thought! But I can't anymore. I'd love to be a bit more reassured that the unpleasant things in life will someday make perfect sense and all will be well, but I just don't see that so clearly anymore.

Looking back on previous chapters of our lives, we can all see that there are some things that won't ever happen again. We grow up. We move. People come in and out of our lives, and sometimes they don't come back in the same way. We go through tough situations, and we know that we'll never again have that certain naiveté that we used to have. Life scars us, and even when we've healed, we'll forever be changed in some way. We all miss things from our past, and sometimes there's not a thing we can do to re-capture them.

So what should we do? I think back on my church experience, and I smile at the memories. I linger there for a bit, and I try to move on. There's not much point in lingering for too long. Why should I? I can't go back in time, and I can't reinvent the situations from the past. Even if I could, I wouldn't be the same person as I was back then. So I pick up the phone and call my aunt. I go for a long walk or a have a glass of rosé. I check my email and reply to a message from a new friend. I go the library and pick up a book about astronomy, or an issue of *Scientific American Mind* magazine—things that I wasn't interested in six or seven years ago. I take in my surroundings and remind myself to focus on what's real to me now, in this place. I see that I no longer need all those "church things" to feel happy, safe, purposeful, and good.

IF I HAD A CHILD
(April 2018)

It's been a year of babies here in my little world. A couple of weeks ago, a friend called and we chatted briefly, as we do a few times a year. When a baby started to fuss in the background, she told me that— Surprise!—she'd had a baby recently. After my momentary disbelief ("No, you're babysitting! Are you? Really?"), she laughingly insisted it was her baby. She eventually sent me a couple of photos of a Batman costume-clad baby boy. On Canada Day, another friend had her first baby. Friends' younger siblings are becoming moms and dads. Older friends are having grandbabies. Increasingly, my age group at work is going on maternity leave and tacking baby photos onto the bulletin board.

For as long as I can remember, I was certain that I wouldn't have a child of my own. In the past, I've been open to the idea, but for a number of reasons, I plan to not have children. I've sometimes thought that maybe someday I'd foster or adopt a child, but that "someday" is generally distant and vague. I do still, occasionally, have thoughts like many other people do: "If that were my kid, I'd make sure that _____." "I would _____, just like my parents did." "Unlike this person or that person, I'd _____."

If I found out that I was "with child," I hope that I'd keep my mind open. I hope that I wouldn't be terrified of what might happen to my little one in this big world, and I hope that I wouldn't be overly full of wild dreams and plans. I hope that I'd try my absolute best to be a good parent, and I hope that I wouldn't base all my happiness on what my kid does or doesn't do. I hope that I'd keep an open mind about what that little embryo will be like as a five-year-old or a fifteen-year-old. I hope that I would allow room for movement, for individuality, for someone who's not like me.

If I had a toddler, I hope I'd sometimes be silly like a kid—that I'd be a bit more carefree and put away the grown-up books and chores for a while. I hope I'd also remember that sometimes it's good to have a long cry. I'd set that important "screen time" limit and stick to it, for my kid and for myself, remembering that it's *real life* that matters.

I hope that I'd inspire my child to be kind, to be curious about the world and how it works, and to be interested in other people.

If I had a kid, I hope that in many ways I'd be the example that my parents were to my siblings and me. My parents taught us that you don't have to be the "most popular" kid, and that it's enough to have a good friend or two. I'd want my kid to know that you don't have to wear cool clothes—just wear whatever you like! I'd want them to know that it's important to try your best at school, but it's not the end of the world if you're not perfect at everything. I'd want my kids to know that it's possible to survive without tons of toys or a big house, and that joy can be found in simplicity. My parents continue to demonstrate this, and I'm grateful for these lessons!

When my hypothetical kid becomes a teenager, I'd encourage her to think carefully about which groups and activities she wants to join. I'd encourage paying attention to emotions and reasoning. I'd remind her that friends and interests come and go, so don't feel you have to stick with something forever, just because it made sense to you at one point. I'd tell my teenager that it's okay to question the words and actions of your peers and people in positions of authority.

When that big day of high school graduation arrives for my imaginary child, I might give a little pep talk before all the celebrations. I'd remind my child that just because you made Plan A for "Life After High School" doesn't mean you have to stick with it if it doesn't suit you anymore. It doesn't matter if you get a doctorate degree or finish a certificate program or withdraw. Do what makes you happy, and do it well. Follow the words of Martin Luther King Jr.: "If a man is called to be a streetsweeper, he should sweep streets even as Michelangelo painted, or Beethoven played music, or Shakespeare wrote poetry. He should sweep streets so well that all the hosts of heaven and earth will pause to say, 'Here lived a great streetsweeper who did his job well.'"[1] I might laugh a bit after sharing that quote with my high school graduate, but I'd also say, "That's good advice, though, isn't it?"

If my child quit his job or his post-secondary education or his marriage, I hope I'd stay relatively calm and say, "Oh? Tell me more." I hope I'd resist the impulse to worry about his pension, his skills, or his inability to get along with every single human for his entire life. I hope I'd have a bit of faith in his decisions as a grown-up, even if I don't understand them 100 per cent. I hope I'd always leave the door open, and if a visit doesn't go well, we'd end with, "Well, we'll talk again soon, okay?"

I'd remind him or her just how important it is to be true to oneself, to have your outside match your inside. I'd remind my child that there's only one person who will always be with you—yourself!—so make your peace with that and try to like that person. Listen to others' opinions and consider them, but also give weight to your own.

I'd encourage her to keep up, somewhat, with modern technologies and such things as social media and the goings-on of the world, but also to be careful about not getting too wrapped in that. *(Look up at the skyscrapers and the clouds! Flip through that June 2014 magazine in the doctor's office waiting room. Make small talk with the barista or the taxi driver. Leave the phone at home when going for a run or hanging out at the mall!)*

I'd remind my kid that sometimes the things we least expect to lose (a friendship, a pet, a favourite toy) do disappear. In the same way that I try to come to grips with that in my own life, I hope I could teach

---

1   Martin Luther King Jr., "What Is Your Life's Blueprint?" Barratt Junior High School, Philadelphia, October 26, 1967

my child about holding on and letting go. About cherishing the happy moments and realizing that grief means we had something wonderful for a while. About not keeping our memories stronger than our dreams.

If my child were to express an interest in a particular religion, I'd remind them to tread carefully in this territory and to not get drawn in because of guilt or fear, or smooth-talkers, or that cute boy in the worship band. I'd remind them about the saying of Robert Grudin: "We struggle with, agonize over, and bluster heroically about the great questions of life when the answers to most of these lie hidden in our attitude toward the thousand minor details of each day."[2] I'd remind my kid that religion often complicates things unnecessarily, and it doesn't always help us become wise and caring human beings.

If I had a child, at the appropriate time I'd gently bring up the topics of dying and death. Perhaps we'd sit together and read *Lifetimes: A Beautiful Way to Explain Death to Children* and *The Tenth Good Thing about Barney*. I'd encourage my kid to delve into the tough, uncomfortable questions about death, to not shy away from the awkwardness of such things. We'd talk about how to live our lives so that, when it's time for that unavoidable chapter, we have peace of mind and not too many regrets about how we spent our time here on Earth.

I plan to head out to Richmond in a couple months, and there I'll meet my friend's baby boy. I don't know what I'll say to him or what he'll say to me, but we'll probably make faces at each other and crawl around together on the living room floor. In a couple of years, he'll show me his paintings from kindergarten class. A while after that, my

---

2   Robert Grudin, *Time and the Art of Living* (Cambridge, Massachusetts: Harper & Row, 1982)

friend will tell me about life with a teenage son. And then … and then, who knows? Who knows how things will develop in his life, in my friend's life, in any of our lives? I'm curious about the journey.

EXPANSION
(July 2017)

My world has expanded. *I'm seeing a bigger picture now. There's so much out there in the real world. My focus used to be so narrow!* These are some of the phrases I catch myself thinking and saying nowadays, as "post-deconversion Tania" settles into a new worldview and continues to let go of the bits of religion that linger. As time goes on, I'm appreciating the expansion of my world. I have the freedom to question, to explore, to turn things on their heads and see them in a new light.

The thing I remember most clearly about the summer of 2011 (the year my deconversion started) is curling up on my fake leather couch in my basement suite and reading, reading, reading. Unable to find satisfying answers to my "big questions" by reading books written by religious (mostly Christian) authors, I decided to … carefully, hesitantly, a bit guiltily … read books written by agnostics, atheists, skeptics, and non-religious or "backslidden" people. To my surprise, a lot of the books made sense. I "got" them. The authors frankly discussed matters that I used to think were "bad." They tossed around the idea that God might not be real, or that the Bible might be written solely by people, or that Jesus might have been less than the saviour of the world. I spent much of that summer on my couch, at the library, and on websites that I never would have glanced at the year before. Early one morning, around 2:00 a.m., I sat at my kitchen table and realized that God was no longer real to me. My world shattered. And my world got bigger.

I've often heard that for many people who deconvert from their religion, the first two years are the most intense. There are challenges and changes that happen for years afterwards, but that initial two-year period is an especially intense roller coaster ride. It's a time of letting go of many things, but also a time of letting in new ways of being and doing.

During that period of my life, a few other big life events also took place. In the winter of 2012, I moved to a new town, started a job at a funeral home, and became involved in an unhealthy relationship with a man who eventually became my fiancé (and then, not much later, my ex-fiancé). Those circumstances quickly led to what I call my "Summerland chapter," and it certainly wasn't the happiest time of my life. As much as I like the town itself, when I think of it nowadays, I mostly think of how much I hurt when I was there. There were numerous times when I thought, *I can't do this anymore; every single tiny task is monumental. Why bother with anything?* Looking back now on that period of coldness and emptiness, I see that my world was made bigger. I saw a lot. I felt a lot. My mind entered places I'd never imagined. Luckily, eventually, I emerged.

For quite a long time after the start of my transition from Christianity, I tried to maintain some of the routines of a Christian's life. That was my life, my comfort zone, my place where things made sense. Where would I turn for comfort if I no longer whispered or scribbled my prayers to God? How would I be a good person if I didn't read the Word of God? Would Sunday mornings ever be doable without church services? How would I think about day-to-day things if not with a Christian slant? The Christian faith provided me with answers to the big and small questions of life. But as time went on, I found it necessary to loosen my grip on Christianity, because it was too exhausting to keep doing what I was doing when it no longer made sense to me. My church attendance became more sporadic. I struggled with praying … then I gave it a break for a while… then I forgot to pray … then eventually I realized that I just couldn't pray at all anymore. My Bible stayed on the shelf. My mind wandered when I played worship songs on the piano. I began to pay more attention to how other people functioned, especially those who didn't have any religious affiliation. I saw that many of them were doing just fine.

For a while, I went to the Centre for Spiritual Living instead of regular church. There I had permission to believe or not believe. I was encouraged to let go of the things that no longer served me. I was reminded that if something doesn't resonate with me, I don't have to go along with it. I didn't have to believe in God in order to be a decent human being. I could be open and honest about the Biblical teachings that were too far out in left field for me. These were new concepts to me. Some Sunday mornings, I decided not to attend any type of service anywhere. I slept in. I went to coffee shops and the art gallery, and I walked by the lake. I saw how other people did Sunday mornings.

Of course, loss and rebuilding happen in many areas of life, and often in areas where we least expect it. For most of my life, I thought that certain people would be in my life forever. I thought that every friendship would be a lifelong friendship, and that although some friendships would drift apart as people move and marry and have children, there'd always be some connection. I've learned that this isn't the case, for a variety of reasons. Sometimes I'm the one who backs away, and sometimes other people back away from me. There are many layers to these situations, and it's not always easy to come to terms with them.

As time went on, I waited for God and the church people and certain friends to come running after me and ask, "What's going on? How are you?" And I felt emptiness when that didn't happen. It really hurt that God didn't show up for me during my Summerland chapter. I thought He was a loving Father. I thought that this, of all times, would be when He'd be there to hold my hand in some way. I had to stop expecting that to happen and start changing the way I thought about my faith. As I began to reach out to other people, and they reached out to me, I slowly started to see that maybe, just maybe, the potential for companionship and closeness exists outside of "the family of God." Gradually, I also learned to allow new friendships to develop to the depths that I'd had with friends from my past. My eyes were opened a bit more to the rest of the human population.

It might be tempting to stay where it's cozy, where the stories and the routines are familiar; and when we do allow ourselves to see more of the world, it can be very unsettling. However, if we can manage to push aside the obstacles—our fears, or perhaps the rules we grew up with—it can be a wonderful thing to see all of creation in a new light. The world is a big place, and how fortunate we are that we can open our eyes to that.

I definitely want to keep exploring.

ALLIGATOR PANTS
(August 2018)

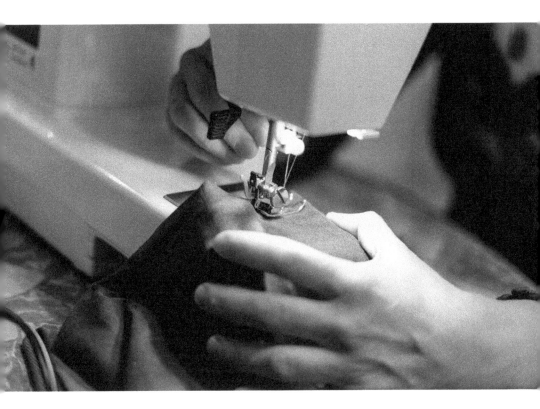

In the bottom of my bedroom closet sits a box containing a sewing machine. I use it every once in a while to hem a pair of pants or fix a seam—no major projects anymore. But back in high school? Shiny alligator-print faux leather pants? A long-sleeved leafy autumnal dress with tons of buttons? A bright red and orange Chinese-style dress called a "cheongsam"? Oh, yeah, I sewed it all, and I wore it all, and I was darn proud of it. Nowadays, part of me cringes when I think about that, but another part says, "Well, good for you, young Tania! You did your own thing!"

A few years after my sewing days, I read *The Five Secrets You Must Discover before You Die,* by John Izzo, Ph.D. He interviewed a couple of hundred people over the age of sixty to hear their suggestions about making the most out of our lives. I wrote down the five points and kept a copy in my wallet for a long time, but the first point didn't hit home until I deconverted from my religious faith about seven years ago. In some ways, I'd been living the first point already—just look at those pants and that short spiky hair—but only in small ways in comparison to what was to come. That first point is "Be True to Yourself."

Ah yes ... being true to yourself. Letting the outside match the inside. Doing what you want to do or need to do, instead of allowing other people to make your decisions for you. Being honest with yourself. To paraphrase Henry David Thoreau: marching to the beat of your own drummer.

Sometimes being true to oneself comes at a cost, whether that's emotionally, socially, logistically, financially, and so on. Yet quite often it's so worth it. I'll never forget the day I dropped out of nursing school, almost half a lifetime ago now. It was the start of the second year of a four-year program, and I just wasn't into it. I'd spend a lot of time contemplating other options and just sitting through class, uninterested. One warm autumn day, I was a few hours into a shift during my practicum, and I knew I didn't want to do it anymore. After talking briefly with my instructor, I walked out of the hospital. I sat at a picnic table at a nearby park and wondered, "What on Earth do I do now?" I'd spent years thinking that this was what I wanted to do. I had no alternative plan, no job, no rental where I could stay, and a fairly large student loan. It was one of the most terrifying and thrilling moments of my life.

I have a friend who, having kept quiet about her sexual identity and preferences for the first couple of decades of her life, finally revealed to everyone the truth about who she is. As she told me bits and pieces of her story, I gained a deeper understanding of the issues she dealt with. She'd had conflicts in her own mind, because she'd also been raised in a Christian environment where any sexual orientation besides hetero-sexuality is frowned on. She worried about telling her parents about her true feelings, and also about them meeting and getting to know her new partner. As it turned out, her revelation wasn't catastrophic for her family, as she'd imagined it would be, and I know she feels lighter now that she can be honest with herself and others.

Doing what you feel you have to do isn't always about a major life deci-sion, but I think it's still important that our actions and our thoughts line up, even in the little things. As I'm reaching my mid-thirties, I'm learning that it's okay for me to express my hurt when I've been treated unfairly, instead of just pretending that I didn't notice or that I'm tough. I can say "no" when someone invites me to a movie that I really don't want to see, and then I can suggest that we still meet up, but maybe we can go to a different movie or do something totally different. When a friend's behaviour confuses me, I can say, "Wait a sec, I'm confused. What did that mean?" And if a hairdresser gives me ringlets when I didn't ask for ringlets, I can certainly ask for some straightening!

It's not always easy to be true to oneself. It can be downright heart-breaking to let go of parts of your life you thought would always be around. I watch a co-worker struggling with a marriage that doesn't seem to get better. My guess might be wrong, because I don't know the whole story, but I imagine a battle going on inside: *This is what I signed up for; this is what's expected of me; this is what I've spent years investing in. But I don't want it anymore. I've tried and tried, and I think I'm done.*

I know from personal experience the pain of knowing that what you're doing (in my case, leaving my religious faith) is going to hurt your parents, your friends, your church family. It hurts to realize that what was once so important—so real, so vital—is no longer so. I know that in many of these instances, I've tried again and again to make things work, to make them go back to how they used to be. But in the meantime, I've grown. I've learned new information. Other people have changed. What was such a big deal ten years ago isn't anymore. I realize how short and precious life is and that I don't have an endless supply of time and effort to spend on everything that shows up on my path.

I've learned that some people won't try to understand your ways. They'll dislike you, no matter what you do or don't do. They'll come around, eventually, or they won't—and that's not your problem. Of course, it's still important to be careful in how conduct ourselves around others – we probably don't want too many people to think we're crazy or to strongly dislike us! – but at the end of the day it's our own peace of mind that matters the most.

My words of wisdom are to do life your way. Do what makes you feel fulfilled, purposeful, rich. Spend your time with people who make you feel happy, not just with people who are "age-appropriate" or have the same level of education or are "cool" (or whom you've known for years and therefore "should" be in your life forever). Pick up the phone and make an appointment with that marriage counsellor, even though you've been telling yourself for years that you're fine, your marriage is fine, and you have no need for marriage counselling. Spend a Friday night at Tim Hortons by yourself, with a good book, if that's your idea of a fun weekend activity. Fork out a pile of money for a trip to Cuba, or to pay for scrapbooking supplies, or to donate to a cause that you have researched and think is worthy. Do what makes you feel good.

And by all means, go ahead and sew yourself those shiny, red alligator-print pants!

IT IS WELL
(October 2013)

Almost five years ago, I was standing on the side of a highway when a semi-truck came around a curve not far from where I was, its fifty-three-foot trailer fishtailing all over the highway. I yelled at the man standing beside me to run. Another man, who was also standing with us, saw the truck fishtailing, and he ran too. My car, which I'd pulled over onto the shoulder just a few minutes before the truck came around the curve, was totalled.

I didn't hear the crash. I also didn't see much of the truck. The tractor was blue, and the trailer was white, but that's all I saw. I remember clearly thinking as I was running away from the road: *I didn't think this would be the way I would die.* After realizing I'd survived, my next thoughts were about my parents—how, for their sake, I was grateful to be alive, because I'd heard many times that the death of a child is the most difficult type of death to bear. I also had the thought that I needed to sleep with my stuffed bear that night, which is something I hadn't done for a good fifteen years. Another thought was, *Thank you, thank you, thank you* ...The words of an old hymn might have also played in my mind that day: *It is well, it is well with my soul.* No matter what would have happened with the truck, I knew that my soul would be headed to a safe and happy place.

I do think about death quite a lot—partly because that's how I've always been, partly because I volunteered with hospice for several years and then worked briefly at a funeral home, and partly because of the changes in my religious beliefs since early 2011.

In the last three years, along with becoming less religious, I've also become less spiritual. I doubt I'll ever be someone who meditates, places crystals around the house, becomes a Buddhist, joins the worship band at church, or helps distribute communion wafers. My guess is that I will remain an agnostic humanist for the next sixty or so years until my passing. I'm okay with that. *It is well with my soul.*

When it comes to death, I've seen quite a lot. There are reminders everywhere. I think often of some of my favourite hospice clients I sat with in nursing homes, in the local hospital, or in their own homes. I drank many cups of tea and coffee as I sat beside them. I waited in many hallways while nurses emptied bedpans or administered medications. I whispered what I hoped were words of encouragement to those who were in their last moments. At times, I saw pain. At other times, death was so natural and peaceful.

I was driving home from a restaurant yesterday when an upbeat country song came on the radio. The song took me back in time to the slide presentation at a funeral—a funeral for Tatiana, a five-year-old girl who died last summer after her family was in a boating accident. She survived the initial impact and was rushed to the emergency room, but she didn't make it. I remember going into the prep room at the funeral home and seeing this sweet child on the table. The other staff dressed her and curled her hair. The casket was small, white, delicate. It was so wrong. It was so sad.

I drive over a certain overpass a few times a year, and each time I approach it, I remember, "This is where Mr. Y. killed himself. This is where he hung the rope, where he climbed over, where the rope gave way." I see the beauty all around the place where he died, and I'm overwhelmed with feeling sorry, helpless, hopeless.

I think of Mrs. R., dressed in her Doukhobor clothing, lying peacefully in her casket, wearing her spring/summer funeral outfit. On the floor beside the casket sat a suitcase marked "Final Clothes." (It was springtime when she passed away, so her winter funeral outfit was still in the suitcase.) I think of Mr. K.'s casket being carried down the church aisle as "How Great Thou Art" was played through the speakers. And Mr. B.'s sister running across the parking lot, telling the driver of the hearse to slow down so that she could give him a can of Pepsi that was to be cremated with him.

I started losing my faith almost three years ago, and not long after that, I stopped believing altogether. I don't feel guilt or fear anymore. I don't worry that I'm sinful for doubting. *It is well. It is well with my soul.*

I have let go of my ideas about who God and Jesus are. I'm not concerned about following every teaching to the letter. I know that my heart is in the right place. I know that I'm trying my best in my relationships. I know I'm not perfect, but I'm pretty sure I'm progressing. *It is well. It is well with my soul.*

I am in awe of life, nature, the vastness of the universe. I lack answers to many of the big questions, but *it is well, it is well with my soul.*

I don't have a clear picture anymore of what my afterlife will look like, but *it is well with my soul.*

I see the world around me, the mess and the beauty, the happiness and the pain. We try to fix it. We try to make it better. We do whatever little things or big things we can to make life more bearable, more pleasant, or more beautiful for others. Sometimes all seems well. Other times, it seems to get sadder.

We see that somehow it is all connected, and we also see that we are in control of and responsible for only ourselves, our own thoughts and words and actions.

Every once in a while, I stop by the cemetery, and I'm filled with peace as I think that this is a place where there is a closing, a goodbye to this world. A feeling of stillness.

It is well with my soul.

CPSIA information can be obtained
at www.ICGtesting.com
Printed in the USA
LVHW010107050419
613066LV00001B/1/P

9 781525 545986